DRUGSTORE BLUE

DRUGSTORE BLUE

Susana H. Case

Five Oaks Press
FIVE-OAKS-PRESS.COM

Copyright ©2017 Susana H. Case.
All rights reserved. First print edition.

Five Oaks Press
Newburgh, NY 12550
five-oaks-press.com
editor@five-oaks-press.com

Cover Art: Graphicstock
Author Photo: Ricardo Andre

ISBN: 978-1-944355-34-0

Printed in the United States of America

ACKNOWLEDGMENTS

2 Bridges Review: "Drugtore Blue" (titled "Survival") and "The Rare Blue"
Borderlands: Texas Poetry Review: "Heat"
Catamaran Literary Reader: "What Is It About Women Who Like Snakes?"
Coe Review: "Hourglass"
The Comstock Review: "Cayambe Valley Greenhouses," "Protocol," and "That Time in Bermuda"
Connecticut River Review: "Detail on an Aerial Map"
the delinquent: "Torpedo" (titled "Smart Bomb")
Earth's Daughters: "After the Bitter Orange," "Long Distance," and "Once This Was Something"
em: A Review of Text and Image: "Drive"
Floating Holiday: "Look"
Fourteen Hills: "You were wondering, perhaps, about Keith Richards?"
Hartskill Review: "So You'll Finally Understand"
Hawai'i Pacific Review: "Acid" (titled "The Acid Thrower's Wife")
Imagination and Place: "Paint by Numbers: This Is Not a Nature Poem"
Marathon Literary Review: "So I go my way and you go yours"
Metonym: "Shock Tattoo"
The Milo Review: "Red" (titled "Garbage")
Misfit Magazine: "Empowerment," "Iraqi Men," "Jeanne Moreau, I Love You," and "Sorceress"
Oyez Review: "Gustav and His Flying Bicycle" (titled "*Of One Who Spent Part of His Life in a Monastery and Part in a Psychiatric Institution*")
Panorama: The Journal of Intelligent Travel: "Soroche"
Pittsburgh Poetry Review: "Bleached Blonde with Spiked Dog Collar"
Rattle: "*Hold Me Like You'll Never Let Me Go*"
Red Earth Review: "Old Man with Beard"
The Same: "Still Life with Failed Marriage"
Santa Fe Literary Review: "The Deepest Wound"
Saranac Review: "Morandi's Bottles"
Silver Birch Press: Beach & Pool Memories Series: "*Don't Talk (Put Your Head on My Shoulder)*"
Silver Birch Press: My Mane Memories Series: "Nerve"
Slant: "Kilim"
Spittoon: "Velvet Elvis"
Sugared Water: "Capra" and "*Tanglin' with Your Wires*"
Wild Horses: "Leaving the Palace"

"Mercy" and "A Guy Walks into a Bar" appeared previously in the chapbook, *Anthropologist in Ohio*, Main Street Rag Publishing Company;

"Heat," "Last Day in Ravello," "Morandi's Bottles," and "Paint by Numbers: This Is Not a Nature Poem" appeared previously in the chapbook, *The Cost of Heat*, Pecan Grove Press; "I Think of My Mother and Father, the Early Years" appeared previously in the chapbook, *Manual of Practical Sexual Advice*, Kattywompus Press. Some of these poems have also appeared in the anthologies: *Bared*, Les Femmes Folles Books; *Clash by Night: Lo-fi Poetry*, CityLit Project; *Like a Girl: Perspectives on Feminine Identity*, Lucid Moose Lit; *Poet Sounds: Lo-fi Poetry*, CityLit Project; *Veils, Halos and Shackles: International Poetry on the Oppression and Empowerment of Women*, Kasva Press; *Women Write Resistance*, Hyacinth Girl Press.

A thousand thanks, *grazie mille*, to Mervyn Taylor, a fine poet, and a good friend, who has given me invaluable suggestions and sustenance on multiple versions of this manuscript and to whom I am indebted for the title and the third section heading, to my Tuesday night writing group, Elizabeth Haukaas, Myra Malkin, Lynn McGee, all skillful poets in their own right, who have also offered feedback and nourishment, and finally to Eric Hoffmann, brilliant artist, who has provided space and love and who has always had my back.

CONTENTS

1. Home
   - I Think of My Mother and Father, the Early Years ... 5
   - Drugstore Blue ... 6
   - Sorceress ... 7
   - *Don't Talk (Put Your Head on My Shoulder)* ... 9
   - Nerve ... 10
   - The Boy Next Door ... 11
   - The Rare Blue ... 12

2. Hourglass
   - Insurance Company ... 15
   - Road Trip ... 17
   - *Summer of Love* ... 18
   - Hourglass ... 19
   - Empowerment ... 20
   - Red ... 21
   - Detail on an Aerial Map ... 22
   - *Hold Me Like You'll Never Let Me Go* ... 23
   - So You'll Finally Understand ... 24
   - Mercy ... 25
   - Once This Was Something ... 26
   - Garden of Stone ... 27
   - Paint by Numbers: This Is Not a Nature Poem ... 28
   - Drive ... 30
   - Protocol ... 31

3. All Roads Lead out of Town
   - Thirteen Ways of Looking at Cartagena ... 33
   - You were wondering, perhaps, about Keith Richards? ... 36
   - Shock Tattoo ... 37
   - Kilim ... 38
   - Capra ... 39

That Time in Bermuda	40
Free Association	41
Jeanne Moreau, I Love You	42
Still Life with Failed Marriage	43
Bleached Blonde with Spiked Dog Collar	44
The Deepest Wound	45
Iraqi Men	46
Cayambe Valley Greenhouses	47
Long Distance	48
So I Go My Way and You Go Yours	49
Last Day in Ravello	50
Morandi's Bottles	51

4. The Ghosts That Give Directions

Gustav and His Flying Bicycle	53
Soroche	54
Heat	55
After the Bitter Orange	56
A Guy Walks into a Bar	57
Acid	58
Look	59
Spanish Bombs	60
Orongo	61
Velvet Elvis	62
Leaving the Palace	63
Sacrifice	64
What Is It About Women Who Like Snakes?	66
Torpedo	67
Juana La Larga in Guatemala City, 1803	68
Tanglin' with Your Wires	69
Old Man with Beard	70
Bushwick Blue	71

Notes

For my maternal grandmother, Mary Zura, born in Eastern Europe. In her youth, having never seen a ship, she considered crossing an ocean and thought, *Yes, I can do that.*

*...Love,
blue. Hallucinogenic blue, love.*

—C. D. Wright

1. Home

Perhaps home is not a place but simply an irrevocable condition.

—James Baldwin

I Think of My Mother and Father, the Early Years

Here's how it starts: They're on their way to the Canadian border, the Thousand Islands, its shoals and rocks.

They are eloping, despite my father's financial distress, her father's disapproval. They are aiming to achieve marital bliss, its vicissitudes. Over cascading hair, my mother wears a hat of bird plumage. The short, fluffy brown speckled feathers spill onto her brow. Her clothes are important to her. Not to my father, chain-smoking unfiltered cigarettes, his teeth already stained yellow.

Neither has much more than a passing sense of how this works, though my father has recently been to war. My mother puts one hand on his shoulder, the other on the door of the green Buick sedan on which he still owes too much; they are worried they don't know enough.

The first night, the stress of the unknown will paint a rash on my father's chest. For now, the sky is the clear blue of his eyes.

Drugstore Blue

I'll always associate peaches with cheap jug wine,
      sickly-wet, and riding around in cars
with groups of reckless boys, with you,
      your sweet tongue reaching to squirm
in my mouth, your hand working the zipper
      of my jeans, my smile encouraging, my eyelids
drugstore blue. The time the speedometer
      passed ninety, I discovered I wasn't hooked
on risk-taking after all, and maybe that pullback
      saved me from being another quiet Helen,
science genius we called her, who never wore
      makeup to cover her freckles, who shot
too much smack and died one night, the rain
      unrelenting—like the rain the afternoon
I dug up the grave of the bird I buried, to see
      if it had flown to heaven. Maggots were busy
at work on the corpse in the puddling mud
      and I ran screaming. When I saw you
years after high school, drooping outside a grocery,
      I wanted to rip at the ravage: drug-rumpled
clothes, your unfocused eyes. You're better off
      without me, I remember you cautioning.
I was, though your words came out watery.
      All I could think of was Helen, carried off
by the same wave. Young love for me meant
      fogged windows, fog everywhere,
everything wet with wine, grief, or yearning.
      Old love means every now and then I check
the school's dead list. It keeps getting longer,
      you must be on it—you're never there.

Sorceress

1.
And maybe if Vivian hadn't gotten a headache
that day, one that drilled into the back
of her right eye so that she no longer could stand
the muffle and clack of her fellow office workers'
typing, she wouldn't have left early for home,
wouldn't have found her husband naked
in their bed with a woman
she'd never seen before. She fled Brooklyn
without a change of clothes,
rang my parents' doorbell,
expecting to move in, at least to be invited
up their too-steep staircase for the night.
No way, snarled my mother, hands on hips, that jezebel
Vivian hadn't wanted her brother to marry.

2.
In 1905, Henry Darger was placed involuntarily
in the Illinois Asylum for Feeble-Minded Children
for too much masturbation.
Later, he created collage watercolors
of the virtuous *Vivian Girls*, seven intersexed
princesses, incorporated into a single-spaced,
15,145-page manuscript.
The day that Vivian rang the doorbell,
I was listening to Snakefinger's song,
"The Vivian Girls," on his album,
Chewing Hides the Sound,
except—it didn't. Vivian called my mother a bitch,
howled in the doorway, long, loud, and hard.
She scrunched up her red-stained dark eyes,
yelled, *You can all die!* And poof! Vanished.

3.
At the wedding of her grandson, decades later,
we're together again, Vivian muttering,
spittle flying, my uncle silently seated at the table

farthest away. *She was always crazy as a tack,*
Vivian says of my mother, who isn't around anymore
to correct her mixed metaphor. The name Vivian
means alive, a curse that is her victory.
She's outlived her brother too, molders away
with her daughter, who, fleeing a husband's beatings,
is glad to have had her own curse lifted,
resigned to have little choice but to take her in.

Don't Talk (Put Your Head on My Shoulder)

Beaches in New York City aren't like
beaches in California.
There are never as many blondes.

My high-school boyfriend
knew how to dance—
he could do the Hanky Panky—and he knew
how to reset the odometer
in his father's Ford. Forget classes;
we spent afternoons on Far Rockaway sand.

I cram-tutored him for his Regents exam,
as he stumbled through English.
I was the daughter of a literature teacher.
He got to this country
when he ducked under a fence and ran.

Right before graduation, we walked
for the last time
along the water, looking at shells
washed up by the tides.
"Being here with you feels so right," he sang.
On the way over the Cross Bay Bridge,
Don't Talk (Put Your Head on My Shoulder)
had flowed out of the car radio.
Not good to dance to. But with waves
nuzzling our toes, he remembered
all the lyrics and his grammar was perfect.

Nerve

How I get a second ride: A carnival truck
wheels down my tree-lined street,
jack-in-the-box jingle
floating out, one free ticket for every child.
I line up for the rotating carts,
have my speed and whirl.
Then I race to Lizzie's house, cover my short
hair with the breast-length blond locks
from her talking doll.
The glue that seals the plastic hair
to the rubber scalp has long ago dried out.
Wig askew, my brown bangs showing,
I exchange my blue corduroy knickers
for Lizzie's pink ruffled dress, because
here's what I think makes a little girl:
long curls, a frilly frock,
and what I already have—bee-stung red lips

and nerve. I take my new place in line.
Haven't I seen you here before?
The ticket man takes a closer look.
That's the beginning of a lifetime
of getting asked that same question.
No. I smile, gap-toothed,
already knowing to look him in the eye.

The Boy Next Door

is wasting away from cancer and heroin,
and weighs less than me.
When he says hello with his skeletal face,
it's hard to look.
His friends come by in a convertible
with fins, a confederate flag
flapping in a hollow tube on the back.
Rebel, the driver,
swigs jug wine and the tires shriek
as he accelerates away.
When the boy next door goes away,
I let out my breath.
His mother leans out a window
in her housecoat, drunk again,
watches over the street of red Tudors,
waits hours for him to return.

The boy next door is the reason the police
visit our home, ask my mother
what she has seen.
They remind her of the Gestapo.
Haven't seen a thing, she chirps every time,
serves them milky coffee.
They come in twos, in plainclothes;
one asks serious questions, the other
jokes around with me.

I don't tell them anything either,
though I know my rescuer-mother
cosigned a loan for the mother next door—
it made my father angry—and
I'm pretty sure I know where
the boy next door keeps the drugs.
The gardens at the rear have secrets.
My mother's garden has roses.
When the boy next door dies, my mother
doesn't cry. She cuts a dozen,
makes a bouquet.
Pink ones, she teaches me, mean sympathy.

The Rare Blue

It was the year of blue eyeshadow
stolen from drugstore displays, tubes
stuck in the space
between adolescent padded breasts.
Blue was a carapace, between violet and sage,
eyelids the color of the deep violent sea,
hue the infinity of Vishnu,
sky figure, delft jar glazed to look like porcelain,
Persian porcelain,
King Tut's stained eyebrows
on his funeral mask,
the mask of my face as I walked from the store,
my crew of girls casual behind me.

We never got caught and never stole
from small stores. The chain stores
could sacrifice shadow the color of
woad and indigo,
cobalt,
cornflower,
ultramarine,
lapis lazuli,
azurite,
smalt,
Prussian blue.
Blue all the way to the brow, an eyelid
tin-glazed,
underglazed,
sancai lead glazed,
oxide blue glazed,
a glaze of blue not born of the blues, but the antidote,
spring blue, *felice* blue,
green dragon constellation blue,
occult knowledge blue,
the eye of God.

We were warriors protected by blue. To the bruise
of blue, we caked on black liner, stacked
layers of mascara, and strutted forth
to the bowling alley, Cameo Lanes,
to Eddie's Sweet Shop—into the fray.

2. Hourglass

*I think you travel to search and you come back home
to find yourself there.*

—Chimamanda Ngozi Adichie

Insurance Company

Philomena calls her workers *troops*—
the country is at war. Mean Philomena
discourages bathroom breaks.
I squirm at my grey-metal desk.
Philomena isn't loved, never mind
the Greek root; Philomena isn't a martyr,
never mind the Roman tomb
discovered with her name. Never mind
I'm overqualified. She's getting a raise
and I'm not.

Days go like this: forms forms forms.
We process claims forms.
Philomena isn't sweet and isn't strong.
She isn't the patron saint of youth.
I hate Philomena.
I hate her dull stare.
I hate her navy suits and sensible pumps.
I hate her for having never read
Wallace Stevens.
I'm sure she supports the war.
I'm sure she recommended I not get
my raise.

Philomena is the first person
I see at the company every morning.
She sips coffee
from a blue-and-white cardboard cup
and hands me the day's stack of forms.
No eye contact, no smile,
no good morning for
braless me
in my tie-dyed dresses,
hands sliced from paper cuts.

If I work here too long,
I might stab her with a plastic knife

from my vegetarian lunch, never mind
the peace sign around my neck.
If I work here too long,
I might become her.

Sign in. Sign out.
I want out I want out I want out.
I want to go to school fulltime.
It will take me a year to save enough.
On payday, the worker at the next
grey-metal desk leans over,
repeats herself with satisfaction:
What a girl wants more than anything
is a good strand of pearls.

Road Trip

The guy who wrote the definitive road trip novel
didn't know how to drive.
He just liked the idea of driving,

and that's how I feel when I run my palm
down your body, which is flat,
like the state of Nebraska,
unrolling Nebraska, as Kerouac would describe it.
I like the idea of you.

A road leads to the whole world, he pointed out,
and I concur about roads—
at least the idea of the road.

When Robert Frank drove around the South
taking photographs for *The Americans*,
his camera was confiscated,
and he was taken to a police station,
where he saw a young girl waiting. He saw
the photograph he never got to shoot,

but it's a phantom in the book. It let him know
what to look for as he completed it.
It gave him an idea—
like the way I have an idea about you,
my smooth Nebraska,
I didn't have before.

Summer of Love

I'd awake to the sound
of radio news, another body
thrown into the Mahoning,
or it would be a car bomb,
a *Youngstown tune-up*.
One morning, the man I had then
smashed the radio.
We didn't have money for another.

That type of place: gangsters,
teamsters, blown-up
or underwater grief. Sometimes,
just one human bone would be found,
by a Labrador or another dog
that was bred to retrieve.

The heat and sweat glued yellow
and orange to the sky before
the mills that ran the length of the valley
bolted their doors forever
and the heavens reclaimed their blue.
When his mouth flew open, my man
scorched the low-lying clouds.

Downtown began to empty.
I pried his hands off me,
and ran away from home.
"Young girls are coming to the canyon,"
the Mamas & the Papas sang.
Everything I owned fit
into three grocery cartons.
I thought I'd never be put back together.
I was just a dreamy young girl,
a girl who'd been singed by fire.

Hourglass

The porter runs over to ask if I want him
to take my photo with J. Seward Johnson's
life-sized statue of Marilyn Monroe
in the Washington, DC hotel lobby.
Marilyn, the skirt of her white halter dress
lifted by a blast from a subway grate,
a scene from *The Seven Year Itch*,
shot two weeks before
her separation from Joe DiMaggio.

Joe gave up on her, the way
she gave up on herself, lonely,
in despair at not being taken seriously.
I don't want to give up on myself.

Let's, instead, eat cake together, Marilyn,
damn the waistline, drink
margaritas until we can't stop
laughing, take our high heels and grind
grief into the sidewalk. Let's steal
Better Than Sex mascara from Sephora
and layer it on thick as molasses.

I'm addressing a Marilyn who doesn't exist,
frozen in place in the lobby,
her dress, those years, when it seemed
the only hourglass was her vibrant figure.

And here's the photo the porter took:
I'm gazing out steadfast, cocky in my choices,
no need to prepare for contingencies.

As if Marilyn didn't swallow so many pills.
As if the dress didn't yellow with age.

Empowerment

My first beloved high heels were an impractical
blue Italian, strappy suede sandals
from a Lower East Side
discount shop—I paid cash and cradled them home.

It was the 70s; I was told I wasted my money,
warned I would ruin my knees.

Still, I wanted any man I liked
to want nothing more in life
than to slide off my shoes.

I painted thick smoky-black lines
around my eyes.
I wanted the gaze. I wanted men's smiles.
I wanted my lips punk purple.

The blue of the shoes played off my jeans.
My painted toes played off the blue.
I thought: I can walk in these for miles.
And I did.

Red

Lack of sunlight makes Shirley Manson four times as disobedient; it's the red hair that combats high uric-acid levels, causes homing pigeons and rock stars to lose their way. Now everyone can have red hair, no matter the DNA. And speaking of DNA, that from a kiss remains in the mouth for as much as an hour because sex is not the enemy. DNA is not the enemy. Scientists turn a dead sparrow into a robot that provokes the living to dance, reanimates the jaws of a dead carp to devour any predatory men. Men are not the enemy, though sometimes, it seems so. The hearts of phosphorescent couples beat together; the hearts of phosphorescent couples beat together like the wings of barn swallows.

Detail on an Aerial Map

For me, it's always baffling,
all that skin against skin,
you can't fit a hair between us,
yet not a clue to what's inside.
That carved groove
I trace on one side of your face,
like an arroyo drawn from
above, a detail on an aerial map,
doesn't give away
anything. You need me
like a tongue needs a second
mouth. You don't need me. And
your tongue, it's not saying.

That's okay. Sometimes we don't
want to see the details.
What are details but fireflies,
disrupted in their habitat,
no longer plentiful when
lighting up the night. Sometimes
their flashes synchronize.
And sometimes a map
is just a map. It doesn't mean
we're flying anywhere;
it doesn't mean we have a plane.

Hold Me Like You'll Never Let Me Go

In the street, I find an acoustic guitar,
no name on it, so I decide it's mine
and learn some chords from
a pretty boy ten years younger
whom I retrieve from a SoHo party.

He plays in a garage band. He likes
my long, ironed-straight hair, how I
remove my clothes, their erratic cuts,
easy to toss onto a chair. For a week
we don't leave the apartment.
He makes no plans to go home, but home
is Sweden, so that's understandable.
I strum and roam through rooms,
feeling like a folk goddess.
"I'm leavin' on a jet plane," I sing.

You ever spend a whole week naked, talking
about nothing but folk rock? But then
we run out of food and being with him begins
to seem like shoplifting. You ever do that,
take what you want just to see how it feels?

So You'll Finally Understand

I'm going to mail you a letter and put a swoon
inside, because swooning
used to have its own room in the home
over a hundred years ago,
couches for comfortable faints.
I'm going to mail you a letter and put a couch
inside, where I will fall back looking
dainty-fem, do what's expected of *hysterics*,
those suffering women
of *problematic anatomies*, who need
pelvic massages, who feel better in recline.
I'm going to mail you a pelvic massage
with a four-story building and add
cumulus clouds because they're pretty
and remind me of cauliflower.
I'm going to cause inconveniences,
like thinking for myself. I'm nervous
about the responsibility; I'm not going
to mail you the responsibility.
I'm going to mail you my animal—
you'll find me inside—and loosen a too-
tight corset that constricts flow to the heart.
I swear, I'm going to breathe more easily
right after I mail you my heart.

Mercy

Car radio on, we listen to the news.
Not good. Never is. War's on. Weather's bad.
A long weekend of mishaps,
second guesses.
Driving home through Pennsylvania,
the old route, Christmas decorations
are everywhere, the America I knew as a child.
Wrapped in a heavy blanket,
I'm so cold that the heater, though blasting,
seems weak.
You're quiet, the vapor of your breath
suspended in the road light.
I have a list of reasons for saying nothing.
Nothing left to talk about—except
you put down our dog, full of cancer, too soon.

Once This Was Something

It's too hard to put things back,
too hard to fix the moment when I
realize even the end has picked up
and gone. Having slept on it—rather,
tossed, fitful and stiff—there's surprise
at the pink-streaked sunrise when
the usual still happens. Another poor
bird hits the too-big window and
breaks his neck—all this season,
feathery little deaths. The deck
is slippery with wet leaves, the dog
by the door, waiting to be walked.
I want to mean it this time,
how long I'll need to stay, by when
I'll want to go; I'm no Athena, no goddess
of practical wisdom. So you wait,
watchful, in case I don't mean it.
Here's the coffee. Here's the milk.
Please, you whisper this morning. *Thank you.*
And here comes that skittish
young deer, staking out our garden.
Soon, your garden.

Garden of Stone

That was the year of the garden, the year
we made nonsense. Arguments
could have had substance—the stakes
were important—
the use of the Oxford comma, for instance.
Instead, our sentences were seething
with venom,
Venus brought to her knobbed knees.

How could I know then you'd be one
among many, one in a garden of snakes,
leathery toads, nematodes?
I wished I could tell you something
Baroque-convoluted,
kissed you long and stringy.
Instead, I had trouble breathing,
locked myself in the folly,
a ruined pagoda. At least once a week
I said it was over because
that's what I always do when it's over.
I stayed,
kneeling among poisonous stems.

Memory turns things like that to stones
in the throat.
Foxglove.
Oleander.
Clusters of stinking nightshade.
There was a garden and then there wasn't.

Paint by Numbers: This Is Not a Nature Poem

1.
18 painted turtles lined along a log in muck-
filled Hitchcock pond toward the end
of when we had our house. Unlike me,
they must be hoping for an uneventful life.
I am Ophelia in the nunnery, mad with song.

2.
97 degrees Fahrenheit; abundance
of fireflies. Too hot
for you to paint. On our porch, we down
a bottle of sparkling wine in flashing
light. My mouth feels full of flies.

3.
Boots in our closets packed with nests.
Live peanut-buttered traps snap shut
throughout the rooms. 29 mice. Daylight,
you drive to a field 2 miles away
and, because you're nice, release them.

4.
Richter 6.0 earthquake (epicenter Quebec).
In bed, you joke you made the earth move.
Nervous, I blame the water pump.
Miss the city, the sociopath in studs
and chains who fixed things, lived upstairs.

5.
224 day lily stems @ 15 flowers per.
I stole them from a highway patch
to transplant to the north side
of our house. Feeling transgressive,
we make dirty love all afternoon.

6.
House sold. *An object never serves the same*

function as its image—or its name. Buyer confides the garden clinched the deal. No further pastoral, we take possession of 5 rooms, urban river vu, watch dog walkers from 8 floors up.

Drive

And one highway follows another,
indistinguishable now that concrete
has usurped macadam,
the desert coughed up its last dust
over the sides of the car: 64, 56, 283,
routes like lottery numbers to play,
traveling east, north, red-tailed hawks,
like chain stores and fast talk,
repeating at every so many fence posts,
remains of animals, as if I were seeing
the same brooding bird,
same blood-matted fur, no more arroyos,
no more mesas, my car moving
where freight trains once rolled,
everything else there is to own
left behind with you in one coiled-up
intensity, your own intensity
rattling in anger, everything changing,
nothing changing, as I wonder
how many road trips must it take me
to get where I'm going, always
thinking just get out of there,
get somewhere else, each departure
beginning with less and less to say.

Protocol

> *The world was my oyster, but I used the wrong fork*
> —Oscar Wilde

For you, the choice is the sharpened knife
or the bandage. The question
is whether you're ready to be cut
or are already bleeding. Stretch out
your hands—let me see. Refuse
to talk with your mouth full and you won't
have to answer any questions.

No, the question is, are heat and spice
irrelevant. No, the question is, how
do you remove an alien object
from your mouth, because the knife
is the only piece of silverware
you should never put in your mouth.
Study your place settings
carefully. Everyone important
to you is either knife or bandage,
so you better choose.
Forget about forks and spoons.

You married a knife, but wanted
a bandage. Then you married a bandage,
wanted the knife. You can't stop
shaking your head in perplexity.
A black-handled knife put under a pillow
is supposed to keep away nightmares.
No, that's a myth. The knife is nightmare,
and yet, necessity and beauty. The bandage
winds itself around the wounds
of your body and you, you try to love.

3. All Roads Lead out of Town

we are traveling
where are we going
if we only knew

—Victor Hernández Cruz

Thirteen Ways of Looking at Cartagena

1.
Old men sit with young women
in cafés. From the trees,
you can hear the racket of grackles.

2.
Outside a church,
a woman carries a metal bowl
of fruit on her head.
Sandia. Piña. Mango. Plátano.
She wears the whirling green,
yellow, red skirt of a *palenquera*,
smiles for the photo, the tip.

3.
A man in cow horns
chases women dancing *cumbia*.
His horns aflame, he whistles as he runs.

4.
In Plaza de Bolivar,
a girl and boy are locked together.
Pigeons coo around their feet.
The man on a bench selling coco drinks
sighs.

5.
Emeralds in jewelry store vitrines sparkle
like improbable icicles, their prices large
in devalued pesos, indecipherable.

6.
Is every song about love? I ask
a fisherman. He tells me about his girl,
how hard he had to work to get her,
moves his shoulders to the rhythms.
Give it to me, he sings,
dámelo, a popular song.

7.
The waves are raging. Seawater sprays
across a jammed highway
along the sea of so many blues.

8.
A report notes: ...*an increase
in recent months of violent crime.*
Outside the walls of the old center,
police are fewer,
valuables should be kept out of sight.

9.
Death is the song of a cricket
in *Bitterness for Three Sleepwalkers*.
After Gabo dies, yellow festoons
are strewn about the persimmon walls
of the writer's house.

10.
In the Magdalena River Valley,
the Africans who moved fastest
found refuge in nearby *palenques*,
built walls of stick and mud.

11.
Chiquita Brands massacred
plantation workers when they dared
to strike. No one knows precisely
how many cried out, were
machine-gunned, thrown into the sea.

12.
Horses and donkeys give way
to cars and motorcycles.
Now only tourists ride in carriages.
Ninety degrees and the horses

are too thin. Soon, the newspapers
will write with outrage
about another dead horse.

13.
Late January, Christmas decorations
are still up. Streets bright
with whitewash and paint, purple
flowers flow down balconies.
Cartagena, flocked with love's fake snow.

You were wondering, perhaps, about Keith Richards?

To this day, I cannot look in the mirror without thinking of Keith Richards; the detailed, almost scientific directives that fill his face are difficult to reproduce. Though it isn't mandatory, a more nude Keith Richards seems like something of a rediscovery, a return to an off-camera, everyday realism, a new minimalism, without shading or striping. Recently, I ordered a ravaged copy of Keith Richards, a crucial accessory, just to see if I was exaggerating. There are baroque recipes for combining solids and liquids to create a do-it-yourself Keith Richards, with three tiny dabs of different colors to create the right shade. What seems different now is this piece of advice: Use only as many Keith Richards as you feel comfortable with. Wait, you must be thinking, this requires a certain amount of work. There will always be women who want to use Keith Richards as an art installation, but having a good Keith Richards is more important and desirable than how many you pile up. As one gets older, less is more.

Shock Tattoo

Il primo? She asks. *Your first?*
Sì, I confess
to illustrated Roberta,
of the triple-pierced nose,
a furrow forming
next to the silver ball on her brow,
the ink black flowing into the first link
of the bracelet she drew on my wrist,
the needle radiating pain to my fingertips.
I follow the line of the Milanese hula girl
in mid-swish on her thigh,
whose colors flow into the roses and
parrots and birthdates amid swirls
that cover nearly all Roberta's skin.
Her goth-red nails
show through her clear plastic gloves;
they match her toes.
I can't look at the gun,
still I'm glad we don't use bamboo
and soot.
Machine, she smiles, as she strokes.
We don't say gun.

Kilim

When the new rug arrives—
its dizzying zigzags of red, mustard
and black—nothing
feels familiar in the room.
Even the dog unsettles herself,

walks only around the edges
of the weave. The oak cutout
in the chair you love so much
appears to be frowning.

It's unclear if this
is the rug chosen in the shop
in Fes months before,
the merchant, his built-in sadness,
pulling out dozens of styles to flip
open the geometry for you to view.

Too many details to deal with,
for someone who ordinarily likes
to linger over pretty things. And now,
even the man you've lived with
for years seems askew, though
that's been going on for months.

Here's the fringe,
one-sided as is customary,
needing to be untangled. Here are
his arms—an anomaly,
their reaching toward your hair.

Capra

I like goats for the horizontal pupils of their eyes.
At the children's zoo, I pet
their bristled coats, feed them kibble
to feel those soft ruminant mouths,
nibbles of their prehensile upper lips.

Touring about in a car near Marrakech,
I laughed when I saw them in trees; they climb
to eat the Argan leaves and fruit.
I like goats because they are funny
when they balance their round rumps
on a thin branch, or race
through a field, then leap for joy.

Tom Robbins, in *Even Cowgirls Get the Blues*,
wrote, *People should go to goats
instead of psychiatrists.* They both
say about as much—but goats don't send bills.

I like goats for how they insert themselves
into stories, those of a friend
whose father kept them, and further back, Pan.
There's Amalthea, who suckles Zeus
after he is whisked away from the baby-eater,
and Heidrun, Odin's goat, who, in her udders,
brews the mead for all the dead Norse warriors
in Valhalla, who grazes on the leaves
of Yggdrasil, the tree that supports nine worlds.

That Time in Bermuda

When the windstorms get abrasive with grit,
when the peculiar warmth of winter,
even in New York City,
means sandals and painted toes,
when a red, yellow, and blue Painted Bunting
spends his days in the park's ground growth,
instead of sojourning in Panama,
I look out of windows
spattered with the residue of rains
and I conjure you

standing on an island road with me,
always hat and sunglasses,
smiling at a horticultural entanglement,
flowers as brilliant as the old Kodachrome colors,

and I remember that night in Bermuda,
the bottle of champagne,
how we shook a tree,
hoping to see those peeping jeweled frogs,
instead getting soaked
by raindrops from the leaves,
laughing until we couldn't straighten up or talk,
me, ignoring my broken foot, you, ignoring
our broken year,
and with losses tempered by a sky
crammed with constellations
faded by ambient light, we found the dark
from the spent day and chewed it up, and then

it vanished in the evanescent full-moon sea.

Free Association

The café where we first met is no more.
Cannoli and cucciddati
line up prettily in memory's display case.

For years, the burgundy awning
lingered on, as we did—reluctant
to leave each other, clinging

to one more sugar high, one more song.
The garden across the street,
so spindly before, is thick with green

and that's how it goes, one thing
thriving, another slipping away.
There's a restaurant, a new name

on the glass door: Freud.
We are never so defenseless
against suffering as when we love.

Where was Freud when I needed him,
when you and I suffered and loved?
His ghost has settled

into that eponymous space,
its evocation of old Vienna,
art nouveau lamps over the bar.

Does he lick his ghost lips
in contemplation of the beef tartare?
He could keep an office in the back,

light his cigar, instruct me, neutrally,
lie down on the couch, my dear, and
tell me everything that's in your head.

Jeanne Moreau, I Love You

In the film, Jeanne Moreau has two lovers,
a rich one on his polo horse and a poor
archaeologist, connoisseur of good bones.
The husband in Dijon is unbearable
in his sarcastic neglect of her.
How can anyone resist her pouty lips,
dismissed by cameramen as not photogenic—
I want to kiss those lips.

Her orgasm, shown as a trembling hand,
labeled *The Lovers* pornographic
until Justice Potter Stewart at the Supreme Court
ruled, *I know it when I see it*, and this is not porn.

I remember, sadly, in an interview, she announced
that sex as an older woman was undignified.
But, in the film she's young, and her existence
as domestic furniture deviates
in unexpected ways: One night of making love

and there she goes with the new lover, in his Citroën,
away into the sunrise, into a revised life,
escaping the death so resident in her old one.
And sex is a *little death*, sure,
but escape from death too,
done here to the music of Brahms.
Besides, her archaeologist makes her laugh.

I don't want to see her die for not one,
but two indiscretions, this being 1958.
What courage she has driving away
from the Lake of Indifference to Terra Incognita,
as the map drawn at the beginning
of the movie lays out the land of love!
Not even one time does she look back.

Still Life with Failed Marriage

I lied, promised I would learn to drive
stick, which you couldn't do—otherwise,
you wouldn't fly to Oslo with me.
When the green VW Bug stalled,
then stalled again, at the airport
car rental lot with the likes of me
at the wheel, I cajoled you, shamelessly,
into trying to drive it, then lied
and promised I would love you forever.
I got away with all of it because lying
was habit, the sex was good, and you
wanted to believe me,
though you already suspected
I couldn't possibly mean it. You hadn't yet
fully learned how unreliable
cars and women could be. Together,
we marveled at fjords, read pamphlets
on ice flow, skerries, visited medieval post
and lintel wooden churches before that neo-Nazi
rock musician started arsoning them down.

You wrestled that damn little car
north because I dreamed of seeing reindeer,
because you still wanted to please me. I lied
and promised this was the best vacation ever,
that when we got home, I would finally quiet down.
Though I never did learn to drive stick,
I did figure out that, for me, going smoothly
was the tricky part. It didn't require as much skill
to come to a safe stop: just
depress the clutch, firmly hit the brake.

Bleached Blonde with Spiked Dog Collar

for Vivienne Westwood

I want the rhetoric. The lyric. The look.
She has them all—her *coupe-sauvage*
cropped hair, tufted. She's an asymmetric
tropical bird, a long way from Tintwistle.
She names the King's Road shop *SEX*,
puffy pink letters, sells punk
bricolage, studs, chicken bones, nipple zips.

Style icon, she pokes a subversive
spoke into the system, sees the link
between *DESTROY* on a tee-shirt
and Pinochet's defeat. But her punks
want revolt just printed on the clothes.
Fuck! Fuck! Fuck! Fuck! she insists
when all they do is jump and spit.
Hey—it's the seventies.

We're each a princess from another planet.
I want to stop traffic, too,
in Chelsea, wearing bruise-colored
makeup and a latex négligée.

The Deepest Wound

In Zimbabwe, I slipped off a ferry,
gouging my shin. For months,
my leg oozed
yellow, a gooey stigmata.

A sales clerk in a clothing store
approached me to ask
what had happened. I think he was
scared I had a disease,
would infect his store.
I will pray for you, he offered.

Someone already had: I could have
crushed my leg
between the boat and the dock,
been lost to crocodiles
in the Zambezi River.

Instead, I wear a scar
that looks like a man's face.
I look at the man-face every day.
He's fading.
He's fading and I'm getting older.
Another year, and like
so many others,
this man, too, will be gone.

Iraqi Men

I need to explain about the jacket,
how the overnight bus from Istanbul
is full—Iraqi men on their way
to the brothels of Sofia, no one speaking to us,
staring, staring at the only two women,
my friend convinced I'm a communist when
I insisted on a trip to Bulgaria.
She sleeps, Quaaluded, in the air-
conditioned freeze of the newly-divorced.
Midnight, the driver brakes
on a shoulder of the highway,
strides the aisle to where we're seated,
halfway back, strips off his leather jacket
as he looms over us, a moraine of a man.
The northwest trip is going south, I think,
too many men and no one here to help us
if/when things turn bad,
        but then he lays his jacket
over me, gently tucks me in before
returning to the wheel and the men
break out their sweets: chewy pale planks
of sesame candy, sugared gummy pinks
and whites, Turkish Delight.
We've got a box of them to exchange,
too, and the men, wordless,
but smiling now, share treats all the way
to the border, all the way to puzzling women
in another city, my only thoughts about
Iraqi men until the almost-spring
when my country drops bombs on them.

Cayambe Valley Greenhouses

I pray for the workers poisoned by roses,
aldicarb and methyl bromide sprayed
into the soil, banned in thirteen nations,

but not in Ecuador. Insecticides, herbicides,
fungicides on four hundred million flowers
shipped to the United States,

on women up to their ankles in petals
as they sort these deceptive beauties.
I give praise for the gargantuan stems

that keep the slums at bay,
more money earned than from anything
except oil and bananas—

$2 a dozen here, $30 and more up north.
The river is the color of butterscotch.
It smells of sulfur, of death and the devil.

The fish float belly-up.
For this land of deformed limbs,
here is the monody:

The god of mentally retarded babies
lives alongside the god of unending
headaches and his two sons, the gods

of twitching muscles and blurred vision.
I cry for the bedridden, the crazed,
their asthma, their broken kidneys,

for this perfect place for growing—
the volcanic soil, the high elevation,
the glory of the blazing equatorial sun.

Long Distance

On Sundays, we have phone sex.
He compares it to biting into an American tomato.
It will have to do until the real thing.

The ideal of perfection. At the market, a woman
yells into her phone—
they are out of the pink radishes she likes,
sharp ones.

She has the pouty mouth of the mistress he had
when he had a wife.
Now, he says, there is no one but me.
He wants me to go there and become a wife, but then
—who will be the mistress? Besides, I like it *here*.
Unlikely we can make this work.

Carp. With capers and olives.
He cooked it before he left for home
that day. I cook the same meal
for one now, every Sunday.

While I wait for him to come back,
I take a course on the origins of the novel
—*deep-breath books*
packed with romantic complications. Realistic.
Gothic. Lovers
separated by the fates and reunited.
I can feel him on my hair and skin. As if
he will return across the sea, Captain Wentworth
to Anne Elliot. As if I, too, can construct a happy
ending, my running breathless through the street.

So I Go My Way and You Go Yours

How often we miss connecting, end up
at the wrong track in the train station,

on the wrong floor, on the wrong street.
Me, waiting in the passage of the Met

where all the Rodins are, while you're
by Redon's bouquet of flowers.

I try not to blotch my face with tears.
Must be some mismatch, or interference

in the atmosphere. What drives me
to sit, to wait near the Bernini fountain

in Piazza Navona, contemplating
the four rivers, a useless street map

of Rome in my pocket, while you're
in Rome, New York, wondering why

we always do this, as you watch the snow
you hate so much fall on the pine barrens.

Last Day in Ravello

At the end, it's an impulsive splurge, thick ceramic
plates that will not arrive home

for three months, a heavy carton of painted
green leaves, Ravello

yellow lemons—I can almost smell their rinds—
and blue. I do not yet realize how splendid food

will look against the bright clay surfaces, linguine
with grappa and lemon sauce

(I will remember to remove the white pith), grilled
pesce spada. There are few troubles

that a *limonaia* won't fix, that the sea won't fix,
that your sweetness won't fix—this is how

you protect me from myself, your fortunate wife.
In the end, yes, all will end.

But, this is no terminal of loss. Here, time
is only wind.

Up in the hills, after a pizza, we look for the goat path
that splits back down to the water.

The twisty stepped route graveled in disuse, we stroll
with cigarettes. On the way down,

I can see the curve in the coast beyond which I know
we will not go.

Morandi's Bottles

thick gesso whites
opaque glass   chalky ceramic
                       architecture
of pure object on Via Fondazza
no skylight   no expanse

form versus the illusory empirical
how difficult to understand
the close at hand   the bottle of wine
you carefully place
upon the horizontal of our table
you're always careful
the glasses   the slow pour
slivers of disquiet dissolve
with drinks and pears
our pared-down figures
elongated   twisted
two perspectives become one
when for a moment life stands still
still life   *natura morta*
De Chirico called it *la vita silente*
silent life
like Morandi you do something new each time
you are measured statement   condensed

temperament   you say only that
you want to make us real
there is nothing more surreal
nothing more abstract than reality
within the studio   a blue velvet dust

4. The Ghosts that Give Directions

In this country the dead travel
as statues and flames.
They wear eyeglasses
and stretch out their scorched arms for flight.

—Tahar Ben Jelloun, translated by Cullen Goldblatt

Gustav and His Flying Bicycle

He wants to love a woman. None will have him,
so his dream is to create
a flying bicycle.

After the mental institutions—thirty-five years
of solitude—in a home for the old, he crafts
wings and pierced sails from wood, metal,

cloth, a shoulder harness from three umbrellas,
a pedal helicopter. Schizophrenic Icarus,
he launches himself, student of lift,

student of plunge. How like loving this is,
the faith, the leap from a cliff—
his sky-high heart. He attests

to success, reaches fifty meters down the valley.
No witnesses.
He soars, glides, heavier than air, aerial.

Soroche

What is the calculus of altitude and allure
in this place where, until the volcano
buried it, the old lake of the Cotocollao
sat at sea level in the valley? In Quito,

the ghost of Ana Bermeo, *La Torera*
(*The Bullfighter*), has slipped from the asylum
to wander streets redolent of guinea pigs
grilled on skewers that jut through their mouths,

and corn: dried, ground, fried, roasted.
She eyes the food, but ghosts don't eat.
Every day, she walks for miles, but ghosts
never get calluses, nor wear out their high heels.

Shaking her carved walking stick, she curses
the fruits of greed—fancy stucco buildings,
gilt churches. She bandaged her eyes
not to see. Not enough in a city so lovely;

she willed herself blind. *La Torera* carries rage
in her large purse where she once carried money,
wears a ratty fox coat and a fedora.
Her cheeks are painted deep dark red.

She doesn't breathe and doesn't get dizzy.
Only tourists do, needing to rest from so much
beauty, from *soroche*, their breath, like that of fish
in the old lake once ash spewed, uncatchable.

Heat

> *The place where you came from ain't there any more, and where you had in mind to go is cancelled out. This place you are now... is nothing but a cardboard box I can knock down any time.*
> —Joyce Carol Oates, "Where Are you Going, Where Have You Been?"

Desert washes make me think of dead girls
in shallow graves—lost—bereft of splendor

their sun-blonded heads turned to roughened dust.
Was this where Evil buried bodies back

in '66—would he go out this far
or are they harshly covered over now

with sprawl—the cheapened ground subdivided?
A deeper maul on top of stolen breath:

lives lived with dearth of yearning to escape
to shed fast the stench of cardboard boredom.

He stood before in a wash such as this
must have had an aftertaste of disgust

choosing already the better next one.
Then turned to go back past Lucky Strike Bowl

past Lube N Tune—past Factory 2-U
past Majestic Tattoo—past EZ Cash

past the Junque for Jesus billboard. Turned back
as I will turn on Escalante—stop

and wonder what those closest to me are
capable of that I have not yet seen.

After the Bitter Orange

Water is life, they say in Marrakech;
the fluid greenness of it
echoes in the curves of the roofs,
inlay of floors. A tourist at the palace

photographs ceiling designs, the perfect
symmetry of both sides of a courtyard,
its central fountain dry.
She can't discern the newer tiles placed
where she's been told the bitter orange trees
used to grow boldly, leafy
when they sunned under open sky.

She tries to fix her mind on pattern
and geometry, remembers
the feel of him on her skin,
the man who doesn't love her anymore.

Water is life. She thinks of when they were
sleepless in the middle of the night
and he would describe how nocturnal
the sea is, deep, eternally moving.

A Guy Walks into a Bar

Not just any bar, but a bar familiar to him,
off Pike Street, the neon of *Renner*
zapping from age in the window,
one hundred percent union made
and no longer brewed here anymore.
It's smoky, dark like any bar and the guy,
who has just thrust his knife
into my girlfriend's sister, is walking away
from the life he knows,
walking away from her life,
which must be dwindling now,
as she bleeds out in her apartment
where she lives alone.
He's exhausted. Keeping together
all of the bits of his life,
the life he had with her,
has been too much for him.
Besides, he's hungry; he orders
another beer to fill himself up.
All those Golden Ambers gone so soon.

It's not a joke.
The guy who walks into the bar
in the joke, he has a dog. Or there's a horse
behind the bar. But this place
is only cheap drinks all night.
The smudges on the glasses go unnoticed.
This is the place
to go unnoticed, the place where
the unnoticed go.
No one has noticed the guy's hands
are quaking. No one
has noticed the dark arterial spurt on his shirt.
This, where everything is most familiar,
is where he goes to walk away.
Doesn't bother to look up
when the door opens.

Acid

Burned: melted breasts,
ear, hair no longer there.
Breath not moving in, not moving out,
braking in front of the corroded necrosis.
Lips fused,
her face effaced by the *sharp water*—

nitric,
or hydrochloric—cheap.
The life that's worse than dying—
her good name ruined,
he tells her, satisfied
her desecration incises her disgrace

in others' eyes.
One eye can't see. Her son can't
see behind her corrugation of scars.
Returned by the authorities
to the husband who threw her life away
like tossing wastewater

out the back door,
his monster wife-wraith,
hidden in the kitchen, sobs
while scouring pans.
There is little escape from
thirty-nine surgeries, the scrape and graft.

There is little escape from pain.
Self-cancellation, its brief flight
in which there is no flight.
The little escape to being the dancing girl
she was, now known always as
the acid thrower's wife.

Look

> *...assuredly drawn under a certain condition of insanity.*
> —Ruskin, cataloguing the Turner Bequest, part of which he destroyed.

And who doesn't work insane at times,
like Turner, painting with tinted steam.
Evanescent. Airy.
Smoke, cloud, haze
viewed through cataracts.
In the center of the field, the eyes
lose focus. That's what I fear:
daze and blindness, that shimmer
of light. How hard,
to look directly into brightness—
one's own bed—to look
through windows into others' beds.
Turner looked, and saw
a couple copulating. Venice *is*
a couple copulating.
Holed up in Hotel Europa,
he worked up a sweat,
avoided the *palazzi*.
Venice is gold and scarlet
run mad. Venice drowning, melting,
structures deconstructed,
a world afloat with 118 islands,
170 canals. Pigments that look infused
with jelly, cream, chocolate,
a dissolving slew
of luminous kitchen supplies.
Leave me, my love, a parcel of drawings.

Spanish Bombs

Fascistas next to an olive tree.
Lorca is shot in the head.
He dared to base a character
in *The House of Bernarda Alba*
on Antonio Benavides' cousin—
Benavides fired the gun.

There's a mass grave in the hills
above Granada,
trenches filled with poets.

In Spain, Lorca said,
*the dead are more alive than the dead
of any other country in the world.*

Kill pay: 500 pesetas a head for teachers.
500 pesetas a head for trade unionists.
500 pesetas a head for leftists.
500 pesetas a head for gay poets.

In Andalucia, Spanish bombs.
The country full of living dead.

Orongo

After the long Tonga winds ended,
the warrior chanted the names of the eight
gods and climbed down footholds in the cliff
where others had fallen to their deaths.
At the bottom, his plunge into the sea
washed away the stripes
he had so carefully painted on his face.
He paddled a reed board,
provisions under one arm,
to the nesting islet, watching for sharks.
Head shaved, nails grown long as talons,
he became *Tangata-manu*. Birdman.

He waited weeks in a small cave
for the terns to arrive, waited
to collect the first egg,
called out to shore when he had it.
While the elders watched,
he climbed up the rocks, hand over hand,
back to the village, the prize
in a reed basket tied to his forehead.
Strong body, delicate egg: He must not
lose his hold on the cliff face.

The swimmer does not become sacred.
The bird does not become sacred.
Always it is the patron, watching from above.

Velvet Elvis

In Britain, stray Elvises play with discarded Christmas velvet, scurvy grass grows in salty verges, and two men are charged with Elvis coursing in Lincolnshire, where the feet and heads of Elvises are being found without their bodies. *It is quite clear*, proclaim the local police, *that something is not quite right*. In Australia, an arsonist attacks two ghost Elvises, a Welshman wrestles a dusky Elvis, and an Elvis climbs aboard the wing of a plane bound for Papua New Guinea. In Nepal, where protesters demand the execution of a rogue Elvis, the government commits to an Elvis cap. Vietnamese officials permit a sanctuary for retired Elvises to remain operational, in spite of public-health concerns. Flooding in South Africa allows the escape of 15,000 farm Elvises. *There used to be only a few Elvises in the Limpopo River*, reports the manager. *Now there are a lot*. Californians petition to end the state's ban on Elvises. *It's hard to get in trouble with an Elvis*, protests an Elvis activist. Elvises on the Gulf Coast wash up with wounds from screwdrivers and 9mm bullets. An Elvis is found in the pocket of a dead man in the Sonoran Desert.

Leaving the Palace

> *Kahina, with foresight, rebuffs the chieftain terrorizing her tribe and goes into hiding.*
> —Berber legend

She leaves the courtyard of powdered marble,
limestone, and albumin to follow
the mournful lute and darbouka drum.
Her mission, to traverse the arid
Atlas Mountains in the distance.

She imagines herself the lute,
imagines herself the chieftain's wife.
No, she sings her dissonant song.
It is her same old silent song.
On the dusty path up, her muscles loosen,
the heat soothes her donkey nature.

In dreams, she is the sun god, Ra,
persistent nullifier of prayer. Awake,
there's no choice but to resist
what they tell her she will always be:
beast, laden now with dangling gold.

Sacrifice

1.
Lined up
at the Great Pyramid—
Tenochtitlan—they
were honored
to be closer to the sun god.
Flowers and dance
prepared them.
Cut with obsidian blades,
they split
with the ease of a pomegranate,
might live long enough
to watch
their own still-beating hearts,
blobs of heat,
lifted toward the sun.
Huitzilopochtli drank
the blood
until his thirst was slaked.
Four tables at the top,
to toss victims down
the sides quickly,
four thousand over four days.

2.
A girl sits
at a table
in a cantina in Queens,
where they grind lime-soaked
corn by stone,
the Aztec way.
My wife...
The Older Man facing her
shakes his head;
a long story ensues.
I can skip the story.
We've heard the story.

The girl's flowered dress
is sliding up her leg.
Her smile
is sliding over him,
her perfect teeth.
She sips sangria
from a jelly jar.
I want to yell at her, *Don't.*
But she has ascended,
now hears only
the round,
pulsating soul of the sun.

What Is It About Women Who Like Snakes?

Every one of us is a braless goddess.
    It's Crete, 1600 BCE,
        panther atop each head,
snake in each hand,
    curl, familiar,
        solidly primal.
            Astarte, lust demon
        with dangling earrings.
    Serpent girls, undulating,
praying.

    Let the rain fall.
        Let the crops thrive.
            Let our nipples rise.
    We are desire,
renewal. We are aligned
        under the naked evening star.

Torpedo

Hedy Lamarr, runaway trophy wife
of a businessman dealing in shells and grenades,
calls George to ask about glands:
George Antheil, crime writer,
master of pneumatic piano rolls—
his hobby is endocrinology.

She's worried; Louis B. Mayer, studio boss,
doesn't want another flapper,
is dismissive of her flat breasts.
He wants a glamour-puss.

Any girl can be glamorous, she sighs.
*All you have to do is stand still
and look stupid.*

From breasts, the talk shifts to weapons.
Instead of a torpedo bra,
Hedy and George invent a radio-controlled
guidance system for torpedoes,
an early smart bomb, voluptuous and busty.

They patent it in 1942. Its parts allude to punched
piano rolls, sixteen perfectly synchronized pianolas
in Antheil's *Ballet Mécanique*
(scored also for airplane propellers).

The Pentagon bosses are as dismissive
of their invention as Louis is of her breasts,
can't grasp a player piano in a torpedo,
refuse to believe
this beautiful woman so nude and orgasmic
running through woods in the film, *Ecstasy*,
so glamour-puss,
could also be smart.

Juana La Larga in Guatemala City, 1803

Tonight I light a candle in your memory,
Long Juana, examined by a court physician
for your *monstrous clitoris*,
inch and a half.
No candle for Esparragosa,

doctor-philosopher who compared you
to the women of Egypt, by which he meant
exotic in *deformity* and *defect*,
who tried to arouse your monster
to assess its threat, grotesque handlings

that failed to inflame you.
Newspapers published maps
of approved-sized parts before your acquittal.
Tonight I light a candle to my freedom,
to the freedom of all women

viewed as licentious—and to those
still not. In your time, many thought
only one sex existed,
some with male genitalia hidden inside.
When overheated by men's work,

they expected a penis would pop out.
Tonight I light a candle to all surprises
of the body. Even then, some called
this idea wrong, said female gender
was determined by flame in the heart.

Tanglin' with Your Wires

When Brian Jones introduced Keith Richards
to the sound of Robert Johnson
and his talking guitar, Richards asked
who the other guy was, playing with him,
didn't realize it was all Johnson,
one instrument, and, in any enterprise,

there are always those who pick up
the chucka-chucka, the bottleneck slides,
almost instantly, hearing
and then re-creating a song.
You wonder what it takes
to have that genius, those long fingers,
for doing things the way
you never learned to do,
because there's always someone
dancing better than you,
loving better than you,
virtuoso who knows more than you,
creates that boogie bass line you can't do.

If you open that someone up, he might
surprise you in his averageness, except for
the fast mastery of that one thing that makes
coins drop down from every corner,
until someone jealous poisons the whisky,
puts him in an unmarked grave.

There may be a trickster at the crossroads
waiting to teach you, too, a Mephistopheles
to tune your blues guitar,
and what can you do but summon him;
bury a box with graveyard dirt, a bone
from a black cat, your photograph—

and then you go ahead, make the deal.

Old Man with Beard

When Viracocha emerged from the lake,
when nothing existed but darkness,
he invented the sun so men and women
could look at one another more clearly,
live without quarrels, or mistakes,

and when his sun moved across the sky,
he decided people should make love
in the light; they blinked their eyes
crawling from caves, rivers, and earth,
where he'd hidden them, lives that lead

to you and me, lying here gently moist,
eyes open to each nuance, evenly breathing
the breath that, long ago, he breathed
into stones, before he walked away,
a bearded old man, westward, over the sea.

Bushwick Blue

The color of the jeans I want:
Bushwick,
a more-or-less feathery fade of blue,
like Bushwick, Brooklyn,
where buildings are so low
that, walking around, I can see the sky,

where breweries have gone to seed.
They're building apartments
on the old Rheingold site. No more
Rheingold, *the dry beer.*
No more Miss Rheingold,
a very white beauty contest.

They brought back both,
cans and contestants,
with *badass* tattooed and pierced
bartenders in the lineup.
Winners could now be
Asians, blacks, Hispanics, or Jews.
The domestic beer crowd yawned.
Rheingold still wasn't cool,
though Bushwick was named
the coolest neighborhood in America.

Is blue the color of Bushwick hip?
Are my nails, your eyes,
the color of Bushwick?
Is the sea Bushwick?
Jazz, glacier-ice Bushwick?
Am I Bushwick, am I blue?

Notes

"Nerve" — This poem is for Liz Frisenda.

"Red" — A partially found poem, the text fragments, strung together, rearranged, and edited, were originally from *Harper's Magazine*, April 2013.

"Paint by Numbers: This Is Not a Nature Poem" — The quotation in the poem is by René Magritte.

"You were wondering, perhaps, about Keith Richards?" — A partially found poem, the words *Keith Richards* replacing various nouns, the text fragments, strung together, rearranged, and edited, were originally from *T: The New York Times Style Magazine*, February 17, 2013.

"*So I go my way and you go yours*" — The title quotation is spoken by Deborah Kerr to Cary Grant in *An Affair To Remember*.

"Last Day in Ravello" — *Pesce spada* is Italian for swordfish. A *limonaia* is a room which contains lemon plants.

"Gustav and His Flying Bicycle" — Gustav Mesmer is the subject of this poem.

"Heat" — This references the serial killer, Charles Schmid, known as *The Pied Piper of Tucson*. He was the inspiration for Joyce Carol Oates' short story, quoted in the epigraph.

"Acid" — Fakhra Younas was the inspiration for this poem. Disfigured and partly blinded by acid when she left her abusive husband, she died after she jumped from a sixth-floor apartment, her fourth suicide attempt in the 12 years following the attack.

"Velvet Elvis" — A partially found poem, the word *Elvis* replacing various animals, the text fragments, strung together, rearranged, and edited, were originally from *Harper's Magazine*, March 2013.

Other Recent Titles by Five Oaks Press:

Model Organism, by Robert Pesich
One Throne, by Rae Hoffman Jager
Spectators, by Rod Davidson
Worth the Candle, by Gary Glauber

www.ingramcontent.com/pod-product-compliance
Lightning Source LLC
Chambersburg PA
CBHW071532080526
44588CB00011B/1651